CW00522120

OXFORD

IN THE 1950S & '60S

MARILYN YURDAN

Students tucking into a pub meal at the Chequers, off the High Street, in 1957. Above them is a 'Parliament' clock, which got its name from an Act of Parliament passed in 1797 when a yearly tax was imposed on all clocks and watches. This resulted in many people selling theirs. Clocks like this one were put up in most hostelries for public use.

First published 2009

The History Press
The Mill, Brimscombe Port
Stroud, Gloucestershire, GL5 2QG
www.thehistorypress.co.uk

© Marilyn Yurdan, 2009

The right of Marilyn Yurdan to be identified as the Author
of this work has been asserted in accordance with the
Copyrights, Designs and Patents Act 1988.

All rights reserved. No part of this book may be reprinted
or reproduced or utilised in any form or by any electronic,
mechanical or other means, now known or hereafter invented,
including photocopying and recording, or in any information
storage or retrieval system, without the permission in writing
from the Publishers.
British Library Cataloguing in Publication Data.
A catalogue record for this book is available from the British Library.

ISBN 978 0 7524 5219 7

Printed in Great Britain

CONTENTS

ACKNOWLEDGEMENTS

Thanks are due to Elizabeth Drury, Dorothy Ivings, Stephanie Jenkins and Margaret Wellens for their recollections of Oxford in the 1950s and '60s, and to Chris McDowell at *Newsquest Oxfordshire*, who supplied the photographs.

This photograph, taken in October 1961, shows a van driver loading copies of the *Oxford Mail* for delivery to news-stands, shops and other outlets throughout the Oxford area.

INTRODUCTION

Although the 1950s and '60s were decades of transition, both physically and socially, in many ways people's lifestyles remained closer to those of their grandparents than of their children. Until the mid-1960s, when the famous 'winds of change' swept over them, the morals, priorities and aspirations of the average Oxonian were very conventional. People still knew their place in society and were concerned with being good neighbours, avoiding trouble and staying out of debt. By 1970, however, British people had begun to expect more out of life, had become part of a growing consumer society and were ready to express their dissatisfaction with those in a position of authority.

Like other ancient towns, Oxford keeps up some old traditions which are seldom found elsewhere, and in some cases are unique. Some have roots which date back to the Middle Ages, while others had lapsed but were subsequently revived in the twentieth century. Not surprisingly, several are related to the university, although many involve Town as well as Gown.

An unusual aspect of the Oxford year is the fact that while the one followed by Town runs from January to December, the university's academic year starts with Matriculation in early October and finishes in late June with Encaenia (the honorary degree ceremony).

The old traditions related to the university, such as the Boat Race, Encaenia and Eights Week, are well covered in guidebooks and sometimes even televised, so a selection of other customs and traditions from both Town and Gown are included in this book, the majority of which take place annually, although a few happen less frequently.

Oxford was once full of ancient hostelries, a large number of which survived into the 1950s and '60s. Over the years many were destroyed, or underwent a change of name or use, and these two decades saw a great deal of change as regards the loss of old ones, the updating of surviving establishments, and the construction of new ones on the housing developments which were springing up in the suburbs. No completely new pubs were built in the city centre, although one or two were relocated or extended.

Oxford still retains its traditional Wednesday market in Gloucester Green but also has an important and historic Covered Market.

Although the city's shops were different in the 1950s and '60s, the central shopping streets were very similar: Cornmarket, High Street, Queen Street, George Street and, to a lesser extent, Broad Street.

Very different from today were St Ebbe's and St Aldate's, with the streets leading off them, St Clements, Walton Street and above all the Cowley Road. Many shops, although still family owned, had a number of branches. At the beginning of the period shops kept a variety of items for sale under one roof, often in a glorious jumble, although specialisation had begun. Another noticeable aspect was the fact that there was always someone available to attend to customers' needs and queries and to demonstrate the goods on display. This was still the era of the customer always being right.

Parades of shops were constructed away from the traditional shopping districts, in new developments like Northway, and precincts appeared. Cowley Centre (now called Templars Square) was Oxford's first 1960s shopping precinct; it was originally open to the elements and consisted of shops built round a square. The West Way Centre in Botley, known as the Square, was opened in 1969 as an extension to Elms Parade, an older row of shops which was built in the 1930s.

Those who know where to look can always find something going on in Oxford, in the town centre, in colleges, university buildings and in shops, and also well away from the main streets. One noticeable feature is the increase in protests and demonstrations in the 1960s, not all them confined to students.

As the 1950s and '60s wore on, some of the most marked changes took place within the home. The population increase and the fact that the Baby Boomers born after the Second World War were reaching marriageable age, resulted in an urgent need for new housing as well as the updating or clearance of substandard accommodation. The largest local authority developments were Barton Estate in Headington, which was constructed to re-house families from the St Ebbe's district, which itself was being demolished, and Blackbird Leys was built by the council in the 1960s and '70s on the site of what was the Oxford Sewage Farm. Other smaller estates, both private and council, grew up on the outskirts, including Wood Farm, Cutteslowe, Rose Hill and Dean Court.

New and modernised accommodation led to an increasing feeling of pride in one's home with rising standards and expectations. The most important single influence on the domestic front was the growing number of women going out to work. Interpreted as being fuelled solely by a desire to earn money in order to buy into an improved lifestyle, it was criticised because it gave rise to a generation of 'latch-key kids'. However, it also meant that housewives were able to have a social life with other adults as well as gaining some financial independence.

Although on the surface Oxford appears timeless in many ways, an enormous amount of building, infilling and restoration is still very much an ongoing process. The 1950s and '60s, however, were a period of outstanding change. Quite frequently buildings would be pulled down as being unsafe, despite their having been listed as being of architectural or historical interest. After two world wars and economic depression the money was not available for the maintenance of the picturesque but impractical.

In one instance a whole district, St Ebbe's, was demolished and its residents re-housed. This involved large tracts of land left semi-derelict until new office blocks, trading estates and, above all, access roads could be put up in their place. In the city centre, the most notable example was the Westgate Centre, itself now threatened with redevelopment.

Although those affected by the re-housing are the only ones really qualified to judge whether or not it was a success, suffice it to say that the case of the destruction of St Ebbe's gave conservationists enough ammunition to fight and win the battle to save Jericho, another run-down but close-knit community, when it was similarly threatened.

Marilyn Yurdan, 2009

1

SIGHTS AND SOUNDS

Bagpipes, Scottish dancing and a first-footer contributed to Hogmanay celebrations held at the Randolph Hotel by the Caledonian Society of Oxford on New Year's Eve 1964. In this picture the first-footer, John Dymond, carrying gifts symbolizing health, wealth and happiness to welcome in 1965, is accompanied by piper C.H. Thomson.

Pop idol Billy Fury must have set female hearts aflutter when he played Aladdin at the New Theatre in 1966. He is shown here surrounded by some of the prize-winners in the seasonal painting competition organised by Wards (Oxford) Ltd. From left to right are: Susan Goodenough, Janet Simmons, Dennis Swanton, Steven Souch, Ann Sellars, Anne Denniss and Stephen Simmons.

Opposite above: Some of the New Year's Eve crowd gathered at Carfax link arms and sing 'Auld Lang Syne' at a minute past midnight, 1957. These revellers are probably members of Oxford University and there is a college scarf in the front row. Those who lived in the suburbs would have had some difficulty getting home as the buses stopped running earlier than they do today and the limited number of car owners would not have risked bringing them into the city centre.

Opposite below: More Highland dress was in evidence at the Caledonian Society's Burns Night dinner, held at the Randolph Hotel in January 1961. The President, Dr Ritchie Russell, is shown cutting the first serving of the haggis, having already recited Burns' time-honoured address to the 'great chieftain o' the puddin'-race.'

Choirboys scramble for pennies in Brasenose Lane during the Beating the Bounds ceremony in 1956. Traditionally, these coins were heated in a shovel over a fire so that onlookers could watch the struggle between caution and greed, but this practice was discontinued by 1956. When Beating the Bounds originated, the choirboys played a more active role, for it was they, rather than the markers, who were thrashed in order to impress on them the limits of their parish.

Opposite above: A Palm Sunday procession at St Frideswide's Church in Osney, April 1962. The vicar, the Revd Arnold Mallinson, blessed a number of palm crosses which were distributed among the congregation. Although in one of the poorer areas of the city, St Frideswide's, along with its mother parish, St Thomas the Martyr, was known for being 'high', as Father Mallinson's vestments suggest.

Opposite below: These ladies are shown packing hot cross buns in preparation for Easter 1969 at the Cadena bakery in Mill Street, Osney. From left to right are Beryl Madden, Barbara Belcher, Vera Morgan, Sheila Belcher and Judy Ryan. Although the buns were pre-packed they would still have been very fresh when they went on sale the following day.

Left: At one time most parishes organised a Beating the Bounds, or boundaries, ceremony on Ascension Day, but the custom gradually died out in the course of the twentieth century. The only one to do so nowadays is St Michael at the North Gate. Parishioners, members of the clergy and choir are shown in 1956.

Below: The River Cherwell crowded with punts near Magdalen Bridge for May Day festivities in 1957. Although celebrations officially begin at 6 a.m. with the choir of Magdalen College singing a hymn from the top of the college tower, some young people would gather the previous evening to spend the night on or near the river. In Oxford, 1 May is seldom warm, which explains why so many people are wearing coats and macs.

May Day was one of the 'flash points' of the academic year when a small number did (and still do) stupid and dangerous things like jumping off the bridge, damaging property, and suspending Minis from the bridge and bicycles from pinnacles. This photograph shows students pulling a float to pieces in 1963.

After the hymn has been sung and the bells have rung out, revellers leave Magdalen Bridge and move up the High Street towards the city centre. The May Day activities must have been particularly well attended in 1966, as some of the crowd literally hung on to buildings in Catte Street in their efforts to get a good view of the Morris dancers in Radcliffe Square.

The costumes that these student Morris dancers were wearing in 1968 are rather unusual ones. The dancer on the left represents the Hobbyhorse and behind him, in the foliage to the extreme left of the picture, is Jack-in-the-Green. These characters, although well enough known elsewhere, do not appear regularly in Oxfordshire Morris sides.

May Morning celebrations are by no means confined to the ancient heart of the city. Most schools would choose a May Queen and attendants, as was the case at East Oxford School where this photograph was taken in 1966.

A condition of sale of land for the founding of New College at the end of the fourteenth century was that the section of city wall which encircled it was kept in good repair. Every three years, in a revival of an old practice, the Lord Mayor, Vice-Chancellor and other officials climb up a ladder in New College to check the state of the wall. This inspection procession, in May 1957, is headed by the Warden of New College and the Mayor, followed by the Mayoress and Town Clerk.

Candidates throng the High Street entrance to the Examination Schools one June day in the 1960s. This caused considerable disruption to traffic and congestion on the pavement, not to mention a certain amount of horseplay on leaving. Nowadays, candidates leave the Schools via Merton Street and are strictly marshalled by the university police.

Opposite above: A demonstration of Town and Gown harmony during the traditional visit to the Lord Mayor, Alderman Alec Parker, by the proctors in the Mayor's parlour at the Town Hall in May 1963. The Lord Mayor is pictured chatting to the Senior Proctor, Mr J.D. Davies while the Junior Proctor, Dr J.B. McLeod, is with the Sheriff. On the right is the University Marshal, Mr W.R. Skinner.

Opposite below: One newly-established tradition was the annual inter-university punting convention. Here an Oxford contestant routes her Cambridge rival during the Ladies' Joust on the Cherwell, June 1962. The organiser, Bernard Walker, the Oxford representative of Harp Lager Ltd, was thrown into the slimy water by the losers. The Harp Trophy, a silver lager bottle made by the Crown Jewellers, was won by St Edmund Hall. The Olympic athlete, Mary Bignall, presented the prizes.

A bicycle-made-for-three was the novel means of transport for these New College undergraduates celebrating the end of their Finals at the Examination Schools. All candidates arrive at the Schools in full academic dress, although they are allowed to shed certain items such as gowns and mortar boards once they are in the exam room. This trio had not in fact taken their last exam as they appear to be sporting white carnations rather than red ones. Doffing their mortar boards are Peter Mynors, Patrick Lepper and James Sabben-Clare.

Exeter College students playing with a barrel organ in Turl Street prior to the college Commemoration Ball in late June 1958. The barrel organ was one of the features of the ball and apparently proved very popular. Big draws at today's balls are likely to include much louder attractions like rock groups, galloping horses or bumper cars.

At Oxford University, degrees are conferred at a number of ceremonies throughout the year, not just at the end of the academic year. As they are not conferred by year or by subject, graduates are able to choose which one they will attend. As these ceremonies are not confined to those who have just received their results, all degrees are represented from the Doctor of Divinity downwards. In this 1960 picture, new MAs are seen re-entering the Sheldonian Theatre.

Checking Ordinary Level examination papers at the offices of the Oxford Local Examination Board, July 1966. The majority of 'O' Levels (which were superseded by GCSEs) were taken at the end of the fifth year at grammar school, although it was also possible to take additional ones or retakes at the same time as 'A' Levels. Most of the checkers appear to be university students doing the checking as a holiday job, but the actual marking of the papers would have been carried out by more senior academics.

A major Oxford tradition is St Giles' Fair, which closes St Giles and some of the surrounding roads for two days in early September every year. Fair days are the first Monday and Tuesday after the first Sunday of the month, unless the 1st (St Giles' Day) is itself a Sunday. This is a view of the fair in 1959.

Opposite above: One of the privileges of being a Freeman of Oxford is being permitted to graze one's livestock on Port Meadow, the large tract of common land to the north-east of the city. The annual Sheriff's Drive takes place on Port Meadow, when all the animals are rounded up to ensure that their owners are entitled to graze them there. Here Shirley Cuddiford gives the Sheriff of Oxford, Councillor A.B. Connors, a ride on her grey mare in July 1962.

Opposite below: The following year a more up-to-date method of transport was used when the Sheriff, Air Vice-Marshal W. MacNeece Foster, undertook what was christened 'Operation Rawhide' by helicopter. The pilot, Peter Peckowski, is shown being thanked by the Sheriff on completion of their work. Of course not everyone has such contacts at their disposal and later sheriffs had to resort to the traditional four-wheel drive.

An unusual addition to St Giles' Fair in 1960 was this Wavy Line stall, which was set up to offer a service and, of course, to advertise the grocery chain itself. This stall was staffed by local girls and did a roaring trade, although carting provisions round the fair was not everybody's idea of fun.

This politically incorrect stall, photographed at St Giles' Fair in 1963, would not be allowed today. It invites visitors to stare at a two-headed giant from Paraguay and sells ethnic balloons. That year the fair was badly disrupted by wasps; St John Ambulance treated twenty-four people stung by wasps and one by a bee.

This rather basic Big Wheel, which looks like something made from a Meccano set, was one of the leading attractions in 1963, possibly because it carried passengers up into the fresh air, well away from all the candyfloss, toffee apples and fruit stalls which had attracted the wasps.

Matriculation is a ceremony in which new students are made full members of the university as opposed to just members of their colleges. It takes place at the beginning of Michaelmas term (mid-October) in the Sheldonian Theatre. In this photograph the 1964 intake at Christ Church poses for the camera.

These children in St Thomas's prepare for Guy Fawkes Night with a huge bonfire made from anything they could beg, borrow or steal, including road signs. The result looks much too precarious to support a guy. The bonfire was one of many built throughout the city in 1961.

This bonfire, constructed in a garden in Balfour Road, Blackbird Leys in 1965, looks much more stable and was probably made by a helpful father, although it would not have done the tree much good when it was set alight. The guy is doing its best not to stay in position and has even turned its back on the boys!

Vandalism was the downside of Bonfire Night and an old-established custom. The owner of this antique shop in Little Clarendon Street got off relatively lightly in 1960, as cars were to be seen suspended from Magdalen Bridge, pushed into the river, or occasionally set alight.

The Lord Mayor of Oxford, Alderman J.N.L. Baker, is pictured walking down St Ebbe's after switching on the street's Christmas lights in December 1964. This was the first time that Christmas lights had been put up there. Alderman Baker was quoted as saying rather ambiguously that he had never seen such lights as appeared that year in St Ebbe's.

These three young boys, wearing their school uniform, were photographed peering rather nervously into a treasure chest which formed part of the Christmas Grotto in Elliston and Cavell (later Debenhams) in late-November 1959. They are, from left to right, Robert and Roger Pollard aged seven and five, and Raymond Berry aged four.

A long-standing tradition in Oxford, as everywhere else in the country, is for employers to organise Christmas and New Year parties for the children of members of their staff. This party, given in January 1950 at W. Lucy's ironworks in Jericho, was very well attended by both children and their parents.

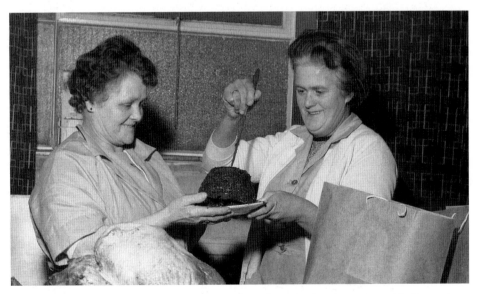

Another widespread seasonal tradition is the free Christmas lunch given to elderly people living alone. In this picture, taken in 1965, Mrs A. Morgan and Mrs E.M. Goodwin prepare chicken soup, turkey, ham, and all the trimmings, followed by Christmas pudding, cream and mince pies for fifty-three pensioners in Rose Hill and Iffley, provided by the Rose Hill Community Association.

December 1965 marked half a century of Lord Mayor's Christmas carol concerts, held at the Town Hall. A long-established tradition was broken that year when the Mayor, Alderman Kathleen Lower, sang the solo part of Good King Wenceslas's page, rather than that of the King himself, which had always traditionally been sung by the Mayor. Wenceslas's part was taken by Dr Sydney Watson. A total of £125 10s was collected for charity.

2

PUBS OLD AND NEW

John O'Malley and
his accordion used to
be in great demand
in the bar of the
Carpenter's Arms,
Hockmore Street.
The landlord, Bill
Woodington, installed
one of Oxford's
first jukeboxes in
the Carpenter's in
the mid-1950s but
this did not prevent
customers enjoying
live music, as this
picture taken in
August 1961 proves.

The bar of the Gloucester Arms in Friars Entry, shortly after Christmas 1956. The 'Gloc' is situated between the university theatre, the Playhouse in Beaumont Street, and the New Theatre in George Street, and the photographs displayed in the bar show various actors and actresses who have performed in Oxford, many of whom visited the pub.

Customers at the Duke of Edinburgh in St Clement's, May 1965, contribute to charity, in this case the Blind. Regular Pat Franklin (centre) had been collecting for a range of good causes for more than twenty-five years.

Above: Mrs Winfred Reading, licensee of the Duke of Cambridge, Little Clarendon Street, is shown serving a customer through one of the smallest off-licence hatchways in the country, February 1965. At this date it was the smallest pub in Oxford and the second smallest in the South of England.

Right: Amanda Grinling and Ann Firbank, two actresses appearing at the Playhouse, help landlady Mrs Pill sweep up the recently demolished pile of pennies which had been accumulating on the bar of the White Horse in Broad Street in aid of the Spastics' Society, 1964. The coins, which totalled £34 5s, were collected in less than a year.

In the summer of 1962, Bert Pill, landlord of the White Horse, and his wife were forced to use a ladder to reach their bed when the stairs leading to the living quarters of the sixteenth-century inn were demolished during renovations. The Pill family had to make this climb in the dark, having switched off the lights in the bar. Bert Pill is shown answering a phone call.

A buffet meal in the Roebuck in Market Street in May 1963, when pub meals were rapidly gaining popularity and smoking in the bar was permitted. Soup cost 1s 6d, Grilled Trout 6s 6d, Mixed Grill was a whopping 9s 6d, Fruit Melba at 2s 6d, or a selection of cheeses at 2s.

One of Oxford's oldest and smallest pubs, the Bear Inn in Alfred Street, is known for its collection of tie-ends displayed in glass cabinets. The collection was started by landlord Alan Course in 1952 and by 1957 totalled about 2,000, with new additions arriving almost daily. Contributors include actors and sportsmen, academics, military personnel and members of countless clubs and societies.

In May 1961 the Bear Inn featured in a film made for Swiss television about a day in the life of a car worker. The landlady, Mrs Van Vlymen, takes the opportunity of adding another tie to the collection by cutting off the end of the one belonging to Mr R. Cann, under-foreman on the Mini-Minor line, while the camera records the action.

Opposite above: Students eating al fresco at the Turf Tavern in June 1960. The student in full academic dress has probably come directly from the Examination Schools. The fact that students were able to visit public houses at all, let alone in academic dress, would have amazed their predecessors, to whom such pleasures were strictly forbidden.

Opposite below: This photograph, taken in the summer of 1963, shows a pig-roast under the supervision of Wally Else, landlord of the Turf Tavern and well-known local character. The pig, which weighed 200lbs, was cooked for eight hours. The actual chef was Alf Weller of Sunningwell, whose uncle was once a famous Oxford rat-catcher.

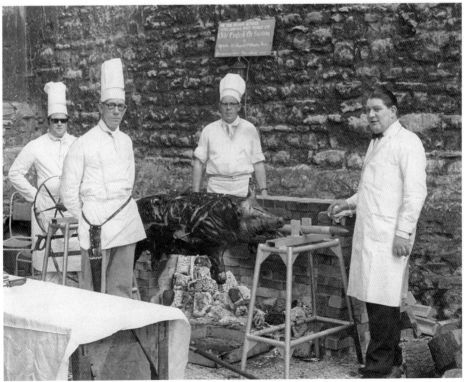

The Hollybush Inn in Bridge Street, Osney, was another pub where customers collected a pile of pennies in aid of the National Spastics' Association. When Oxford United striker, Tony Jones, knocked down this mammoth pile in April 1964, the total was found to be £45 12s 2d. Over six years the Hollybush raised nearly £206 in pennies.

At one time the Jericho House in Walton Street had this unusual sign with a Biblical quotation. Now called the Jude the Obscure, the pub's name still keeps its association with the writer Thomas Hardy, who called the area Beersheba in his novel.

January 1965: the Bulldog on this pub sign in St Aldate's faces towards Christchurch Meadows, the proposed site of the controversial Meadow Road route which never materialised. The reverse of the sign showed a university constable, known as a Bulldog, in pursuit of an undergraduate. The pub was formerly known as the New Inn and is now the Hobgoblin.

The ancient Mitre Hotel is better known today for its restaurant, but it was once a famous coaching inn. The Mitre's rooms, which have been converted into living accommodation for its owners, Lincoln College, had their own names. This picture shows the Castle Room as it was in 1957, complete with Tudor fireplace, wood-panelling and period furnishings.

Below the main rooms of the Mitre is an even older cellar which was used as a bar called the 'Monks' Retreat', where performances, mainly by folksingers, would be held. In this photograph, taken in 1964, the contemporary chairs contrast with the rest of the décor, and the spiral staircase was a definite hazard.

Opposite above: The Deputy Lord Mayor of Oxford, Alderman P.S. Spokes, who was a noted antiquarian and local historian, used to show interested groups round parts of old Oxford. This group, photographed in the cellars of the Mitre, are members of the Oxford Architectural and Historical Society who visited in 1969. They also saw the plate room at the Town Hall, where the city's silver and gold treasures and its ancient charters are housed.

Opposite below: Mr P. Lecamp, chef at the now demolished Abingdon Arms in Market Street, poses with a decorated boar's head which he had prepared for the pub's customers in December 1955. A better known example of this highly specialised dish has been the main feature at the Queen's College every Christmas for centuries and even has its own carol to accompany its entry into the college dining hall.

The Carpenter's Arms in Hockmore Street, Cowley, shown here in 1961, once acted as a community centre for the district. It was the headquarters of Cowley United Football Club and Headington Silver Band, as well as hosting darts, shove ha'penny and Aunt Sally teams and children's dancing classes. The hall, which could be let out for functions, and the pleasant garden, were some of Cowley's main amenities when it was still a separate village.

The façade of the Swan and Castle at No. 5 New Road, photographed in the 1950s. New Road and Castle Street were drastically rebuilt in the 1970s, when several small local pubs like this one disappeared from the city centre. Hall's Brewery, which supplied the Swan and Castle, lasted much longer, but it too eventually closed and the site became part of the rebuilding of the West End, a complex of bars, restaurants and housing.

The tiny Rat Hole (properly the Crown) was at No. 182 Cowley Road. Its sign showed a learned and rather supercilious rodent, peering over his specs. Standing next to a book bearing the crest of the university, he clutched a bottle of Double Diamond, which, as everyone knew, worked wonders. The 'Rattie' has since been superseded by the Brickworks.

The Black Horse Inn was a Botley landmark until its closure in May 1969. Before the pub was sold by Ind Coope (Oxford and West Ltd) to local builders and contractors Frederick J. Minns and Co. Ltd, the Hancox family had held the licence for well over half a century.

The Albert Arms in Albert Street, St Ebbe's, was named after Albert, Duke of Clarence, not his more famous grandfather. It became a public house in 1870 and in the middle of the last century was home to a foul-mouthed parrot named Billy. When the Albert Arms was demolished in 1965, Billy relocated to the Vine at Cumnor.

The Pheasant, an ancient pub on the corner of Keble and Banbury Roads, is seen here during demolition in January 1957. The pub's owner, St John's College, had obtained permission from Oxford City Council to turn the site into offices.

Owners of the site of the Paviers' Arms in Castle Street included Godstow Nunnery, Osney Abbey, and Christ Church, who leased it to Morrell's Brewery and then to Morland's. The stone archway just visible on the left of the building came from Osney Abbey. When the Paviers' closed in 1968, the archway was removed to College Farm, Merton.

This picture of the Farriers' Arms, situated on the corner where the Abingdon Road turns to cross the Red Bridge, was taken in June 1963 when it was under threat due to road widening. This decision provoked a good deal of criticism but the Farriers' was demolished nevertheless.

Although numerous pubs were being closed all over the city, new ones were opening up. This photograph shows first drinks being served at the first post-war pub, The Cavalier in Copse Lane, New Marston, in August 1956. Serving the Mayor, Alderman W.J. Allaway, is the Hon. Peter Remnant, MP, chairman of Hall's Oxford Brewery Ltd.

The District Manager of Simmonds' Brewery, Mr G.L. Hardwick, fills pint glasses to toast the workmen on completion of a new public house, the Fairview Inn in Glebelands, Headington, in May 1959. This alcoholic acknowledgement followed a time-honoured practice which took place when the highest point of a new building was finished.

Left: This picture was taken just before the pub first opened its doors on 12 December 1962, when the licensees were Mr and Mrs Ernest Hanks.

Below: Mr J.H.E. Guest of Ind Coope (Oxford and West) is shown taking part in the traditional 'topping out' ceremony, the pub on this occasion being the Bull-Nosed Morris on the Watlington Road, Blackbird Leys, when the last part of the building was completed in December 1966.

3

SHOPS AND SHOPPING

In October 1957, the *Oxford Mail* produced a 12-page supplement covering the opening of the new Woolworth's store at 52-53 Cornmarket, which was billed at the time as 'the most modern Woolworth store in the country'. Offering a whole new shopping experience it must have posed a serious threat to small, family-owned businesses.

A long-established trading site is the Covered Market, which stretches between Market Street and the High Street. Opened in 1774 to ease congestion in the streets and give shelter to shoppers and traders, it has expanded over the years. Note the sawdust on the floor to absorb blood from the butcher's shop, E. Gibbard & Son, seen here in November 1955.

In 1966 male fashion at Shepherd and Woodward, perhaps better known as makers of academic dress, catered for customers aged nine years upwards. Apart from classic designs, stock included well-cut jeans and trendy button-down denim shirts. A director of the firm stated that, 'We realise that The Beatles and Herman's Hermits have done our trade a lot of good.'

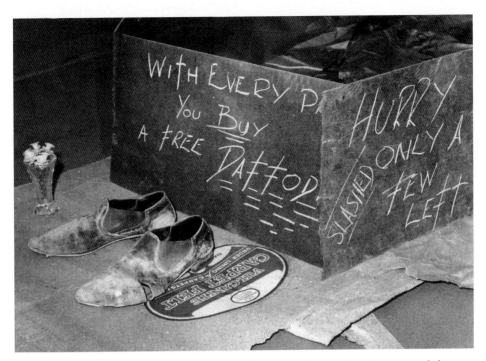

Workmen rebuilding Salisbury's, a leather goods shop in Cornmarket Street, staged this impromptu window display in 1963. It drew plenty of attention with its offer of two very dilapidated shoes. A board behind them read: 'With every pair you buy, a free daffodil. Hurry only a few left.'

The exterior of the newly-built Woolworth's in 1963. The site had previously been occupied by the famous Clarendon Hotel, one of the city's best-known landmarks which was closed at the beginning of the Second World War. This branch has in its turn given way to the Clarendon Centre.

The interior of Woolworth's, crammed with gift ideas, a few days before Christmas 1964. The display of merchandise is quite chaotic and some of the soft toys must have ended up on the floor.

Another shot of a crowded Woolworth's, this time in 1960, when it was possible to buy just about anything from the store. However, the positioning and small number of tills must have been very tempting to shoplifters. One or two customers can be seen trying to attract the attention of the sales staff, while others are patiently waiting their turn.

No city centre would be complete without a Marks & Spencer. This picture shows work in progress in 1961, when a number of old shops in Market Street and Cornmarket were demolished to make way for the new store on the corner. This crane proved more trouble than it was worth when it blocked the streets for the best part of a day.

This well-stocked toy department was located in the Co-op Sports Shop, which moved into Cornmarket in 1957. At that time hula-hoops were very much in fashion, although more traditional toys like teddy bears and other soft toys were still in demand. The scooters on the left are very basic in comparison with today's models.

Opposite above: It is often said that Marks & Spencer is a firm that treats its staff well. In February 1962, while the construction work was still going on, a comfortable roof-top canteen was constructed for the workmen. Shown awaiting the invasion of hungry workers are Mrs M. Townsend, Mrs P. Belcher and Mrs M. Bowler.

Opposite below: Another leading retailer was the Oxford Co-operative Society, which had specialist shops dotted throughout the city centre as well as smaller ones in the suburbs. In the spring of 1957, this new household store was opened after alterations costing nearly £100,000. Here is the Mayfair Hairdressing Salon, the first ladies' hairdressing department to be opened by the Co-operative Society in the city centre.

The newly-opened Regency Corsetry Salon displays what appear to be very uncomfortable foundation garments. The Co-op had its own brand of support garments called Desbeau. Despite this attractive display, many older ladies still patronised corsetieres who worked from their own homes.

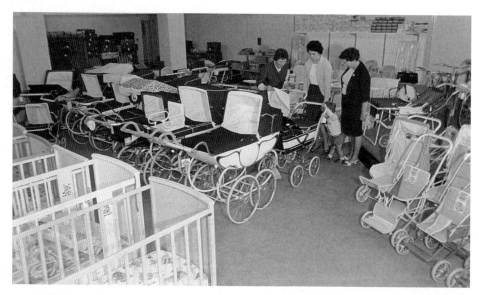

In 1966 the Co-op's nursery department stocked heavyweight prams and pushchairs, which are very different from their modern equivalents. The ladies in the photograph are examining one of the newer types, which had a removable carrycot but would still have been difficult to get on or off a bus.

Two smiling hostesses welcome shoppers
with a demonstration of the usefulness of
the escalators to transport buyers from one
department to another in the main Co-op store
in 1960. It took a little courage to step onto a
moving staircase, although they were a definite
improvement on puffing up flights of stairs or
crowding into stuffy enclosed lifts.

A real innovation was the self-service machine,
described as 'a 6-foot tall robot who serves
night and day', which was installed behind
the Co-op's electrical store in George Street in
1962 at a cost of £1,675. Notice the range of
products on offer and the very desirable prices
– and it even gave change!

This arcade led to the Oxford Drug Company Ltd, whose premises were given a facelift in 1959. A wall was knocked down in order to combine it with its neighbour, H. Boswell and Co., to provide a larger walk-round store. The store, which is still trading as Boswell's of Oxford, is one of the oldest established in the city.

The Oxford Drug Company's cosmetics counter ready for Christmas 1961. The store offered presents for all the family, including a box containing three tablets of picture soap, advertised as 'ideal for any child'. By that time, says the *Oxford Times*, 'The men are shy no more' about buying perfume and make-up for the women in their lives.

In 1962, the ground floor of the newly-expanded Boswell's sold everything from cutlery to handbags and bedding to silverware. The assistants wore smart overalls, while the suited gentleman on the right is a floor-walker poised ready to assist shoppers find the items they are looking for.

Another sizeable department store was Webber's, which occupied a large site on the north side of the High Street, around and above the Covered Market. This view of its 'magnificent redesigned lingerie department', which had twelve fitting rooms, was taken in 1960.

Webber's newly-opened shoe salon sold every kind of female footwear, from stiletto heels to babies' booties. Elegant models in black or taupe cost 79s 11d a pair while those with a satin bow and 'mildly-pointed toe' cost 59s 11d. The most exotic colour that year was 'a vivid shade of purple called "passion"'.

In November 1964, the *Oxford Mail* ran a feature on shopping in St Aldate's in which it observed that this could be a 'pleasant and varied excursion for mother and family'.

These two rather hesitant browsers are looking at the treasures on offer in the St Aldate's branch of the Junk Shop, an old curiosity shop which looked more like a pawnbroker's, in November 1964. The owner had another shop in Castle Street.

One business which operated for 105 years in St Ebbe's was F. Cape & Co., which closed in 1972. Founded in 1872 by Faithful Cape, who sold it to Henry Lewis in 1897, it had branches in Cowley Road, Walton Street and Headington. When the last shop was closed, some of its fittings were reassembled in the Museum of Oxford as an important part of the city's past.

This view of the west side of St Ebbe's in 1964, looking towards Queen Street, includes G.R. Cooper (Oxford) Ltd, household department store and builders' merchants; Braham and Co., antique dealers at the Utility Shop and Cooper's electrical department.

Further down St Ebbe's was P.E. Davis Ltd, furniture dealers at Numbers 23, 24-26 and 27, next door to Dunrite shoe repairers. Although this and the following two photographs formed part of an *Oxford Mail* feature on Christmas shopping in 1964, none of the businesses shown looks very seasonal.

North Parade in 1959. This shopping suburb met the needs of local shoppers with a butcher, baker, grocers and general stores, and even a mini-supermarket. The Rose and Crown pub at No. 14 is still in existence, but the shops have since been replaced by more upmarket businesses.

Opposite above: This 1964 view of the east side of St Ebbe's, looking south, shows Davey Brothers, furnishers; Singer Sewing Machines; G.T. Jones & Co. Ltd, wine merchants; Shirley Smith, Dry Cleaners; Radio Rentals; Chiltern Cleaners; and Ivor Fields' photographic shop.

Opposite below: On the other side of town, St Clement's also had a comprehensive range of local shops so that its residents had little need to cross Magdalen Bridge for their everyday shopping. May's stores originated as a hardware business founded in 1919. Specialising in cookware, crockery and glassware, it also sold Christmas decorations and stationery, as this photograph from 1963 shows.

Dorothy's in Elms Parade, Botley, seen here crammed full with baby-wear, toys, haberdashery, linens and foundation-wear in 1963. The shops in Elms Parade, fronting the Botley Road, were built in the 1930s, well before the rest of the West Way shopping precinct, of which it is now a part.

Opposite above: Warland's Cycles on the Botley Road sold a whole range of bikes, from fairy cycles to full-size men's models. Along with the bikes and their accessories, an assortment of household items, including large saucepans, was offered for sale, as can be seen on the wall behind the shopkeeper.

Opposite below: The Home Linens shop on the Cowley Road sold a lot more than just bed linen and tablecloths. Here is its aptly-named Stork Shop in 1964. The buggy-type pram on the top shelf must have been much easier to manoeuvre than the tall, heavy prams which were more common at the time.

In 1958 an *Oxford Mail* supplement announced that East Oxford had 'Shops that set the Style,' something which may come as a surprise to those who know the area today when it is noted for its large number of restaurants. Here is Woolcraft of Oxford, with owner Mrs Kathleen Nix on the right.

The Emily Summersell shop in Cowley Road, pictured here in 1963. Another Summersell business at that time was a tailoring establishment in Walton Street. Customers could happily browse the shelves which contained everything from shopping bags to ladies' waist slips for only 4s 11d!

Deaney's on the Cowley Road stocked just about everything imaginable relating to cycling and biking. Its mopeds and motorbikes must have made it heaven for young men and you can nearly smell the plastic and new rubber in this picture taken in 1963.

The parade of shops in Westlands Drive, Northway Estate, December 1962. The shops included a post office inside Harmsworth's newsagent and tobacconist's business, Boiteux's hardware shop, Gay's drapers, the usual suburban branch of the Co-op, Dean's drug stores, Cooke's greengrocery, Cock's grocers, Balls Brothers' wine merchants, Berry's the bakers and David's hairdressers. In those days it was safe to leave babies in their prams outside shops.

4

EVENTS

A well-known Oxford character, Jimmy Dingle, was a great fundraiser for charity, the Radcliffe Infirmary being one of his favourite causes. Jimmy is shown on his 65th birthday in May 1950, when he got married for a second time to Miss Edith Matthews, aged 45, at St Mary Magdalen Church. The crowds of well-wishers brought the traffic to a halt.

This undated photograph shows Jimmy Dingle in his working clothes, which consisted of full evening dress, including white scarf and spats. On this occasion he was judging a Guy Fawkes competition at the Super Cinema, where there appears to have been only four contenders for the title. The announcement on the board implies that the construction of guys was an exclusively male activity, which was far from being the case.

A new era in Oxford street-cleaning began in July 1952 when an electrical vehicle was introduced. In one day its five-man team could clean an area equal to that covered by a one-man trolley in a week. Although still primitive by today's standards, elsewhere rubbish was still being collected in horse-drawn carts.

Members of the 6th Oxon (Oxford City Battalion) Home Guard 22 Rifle Team, winners of the Oxfordshire Winter League Division VIII contest in 1954, must have been more proficient than the soldiers in *Dad's Army*. Shown standing from left to right are Sgt P.H. Ponting, CSM P.W. Cambray, Second Lt F. Parker and CSM E.J. Ford, with coach RSM P. Barltrop in the centre.

Members of the RAF march down St Giles' on their way to St Aldate's Church for a Battle of Britain service in September 1957. The parade stretches back a long way and is holding up a double-decker bus. On this occasion the WRAF do not seem to have been represented, although they may have already marched past and out of the picture.

One unusual sight in the summer of 1954 was the departure of teams of Church Army crusaders to eight seaside towns all over England. The picture shows some of them arriving at Christ Church Cathedral for a commissioning service, after which they dispersed to work in more than thirty-two parishes in and around Oxford.

Opposite above: Chipperfield's Circus came to town in October 1954, when it stopped the traffic in High Street. The elephants, together with their young fans, are shown passing the Queen's College. Chipperfield's used to spend the winter months when they were off the road at Heythrop near Chipping Norton, and so were, in a sense, local.

Opposite below: A lone policeman stands guard over the remains of one of the dining rooms forming part of the Clarendon Restaurant in George Street, which were badly damaged by fire in June 1966. The restaurant was above No. 14 George Street, where Bella Italia is now.

72

All aboard for the Inland Waterways Association annual outing in September 1955. There are numerous locks with lock-keepers' cottages along the Thames and this must have given quite a sense of community. The dachshund to the left of the picture seems unsure if it really wants to make this trip.

Opposite above: This photograph was taken during a historic visit to Oxford by Russian leaders Bulgarin and Kruschov in April 1956, during the Cold War. Huge crowds packed the far end of Broad Street as this picture, taken outside the Bodleian Library, shows. Note the climber risking life and limb on the exterior of the New Bodleian on the right of the photograph.

Opposite below: The motorcade is shown coming up St Aldate's towards Carfax. The crowd of spectators spilling out onto the road is made up of a surprising number of ordinary people as well as photographers and journalists.

In November 1957, twenty-five Teddy Boys were jointly charged with using threatening behaviour and obstructing the footpath in Cornmarket Street by walking shoulder-to-shoulder, forcing pedestrians to walk in the road or jump into shop doorways. Most of the youths were fined £4 each and bound over to be of good behaviour for a year in the sum of £25.

Opposite above: Protestors demonstrating against the British Government's action during the Suez Crisis when Egypt nationalized the Suez Canal, took to the streets of Oxford in November 1956. Some of the slogans are still very relevant today.

Opposite below: Workmen and management celebrate the completion of the highest point of the new City Motors showroom in the Botley Road in April 1959 with a pint. A black flag had previously been hoisted to indicate to the owners that beer should be provided for the workmen to toast their achievement. On the right is Deputy Managing Director, Mr V.N.F. Jones.

Dressed in their Sunday best, members of the women's section of the Oxford and District Licensed Victuallers' Protection Association pose by their coach before setting off on a four-day tour, which included Scotland.

Opposite above: This outdoor service of dedication was held on the site of the new Congregational church in Collinwood Road, Risinghurst, in June 1958. One of the ways to raise money for its construction was a resourceful 'Buy a Brick' scheme, the brainchild of the minister, Revd T.C. Stiff. The church took about ten years to complete.

Opposite below: A student 'Ban Polaris' protest group gathered at the Martyrs' Memorial, February 1961. This photograph shows some of the 100-strong Oxford contingent before they left to join a sit-down protest against the US Polaris agreement, outside the Ministry of Defence, in London. The *Oxford Mail* described the demonstration as 'the first in a campaign of non-violent civil disobedience against weapons of mass destruction'.

This Victorian horse-drawn fire engine and its crew were filmed leaving the fire station (when it was still in George Street) as part of the BBC television programme *Blue Peter* in September 1964. Modern fire appliances are based in the present fire station in Rewley Road.

Above: The urge to protest was not confined to students or even to men. Women protesters wearing winkle-pickers, pushing prams and carrying placards for and against a range of causes, marched across Magdalen Bridge as part of the Labour Day parade on 1 May 1963.

Right: Plenty of new sights, sounds and smells for these holiday-makers leaving Oxford station in July 1963. This family's holdall and battered cardboard suitcase, complete with string and Father's plastic mac, are a far cry from today's designer luggage. However unsophisticated the scene, it's certain that holidays in the 1950s and '60s were enjoyed just as much as present-day ones.

Shoppers waited outside the locked doors of Boots the Chemist in Cornmarket Street while police searched the building for a bomb in 1964. Fortunately, they were unable to find one. This was the second bomb hoax in two days. An anonymous caller had rung the police the day before to tell them that a bomb had been planted in Ward's store in Park End.

This photograph of Ringo, George and John was taken after The Beatles had finished dinner at Brasenose College and were on their way for drinks at the exclusive Vincent's Club. It's clear that John has caught sight of the photographer but George and Ringo are unaware of him. Paul is somewhere out of sight.

The crowd of fans being held back by good-natured policemen are waiting to welcome The Beatles to Oxford in March 1964. The group had been in the city as part of a campaign by then student Jeffrey Archer to raise £1 million.

At Christmas 1964, pupils from Redefield School delivered about 140 parcels of tea and biscuits to elderly people on the Blackbird Leys estate. The money to pay for these gifts was raised by a carol-singing tour of the estate, Bingo in the Community Centre, and collections made around the estate by around sixty schoolchildren, their parents and members of the City of Oxford Junior Silver Band.

At least a couple of men took part in the Oxford Co-operative Society's cooking competition held at their Cowley Road store in 1966. It was part of a Danish Bacon promotion and contestants were judged on their ability to cook bacon, tomatoes, eggs and mushrooms. The winner was Mrs Dooley, shown on the far right.

In a competition to find the best-run lock on the River Thames, Osney Lock was judged the winner in the summer of 1967. Lock-keeper J.C.W. Jeffrey is shown beside his array of colourful bedding plants. Today, the lock-keepers' cottages on the Thames continue to brighten up the riverside.

Pop singer turned actor Tommy Steele is shown putting a whole sixpence into a St John Ambulance Brigade collecting tin in February 1967, during their Appeal Year. With Tommy, who was filming *Half a Sixpence* locally, are St John's cadets Ann Buckingham, Isabel Grant and Nurse Jane Porter.

The Lord Mayor, Alderman Frank Pickstock, hands over a 20lb Christmas pudding to the Matron of Townsend House Home, Miss M. Gillespie, in December 1967. With them are Australian Golden Girl Barbara Bowles and Alderman T.G. Meadows. The pudding was presented annually by the Australian High Commission on behalf of the Australian Dried Fruits Board.

During a one-day protest strike by the AEU, members from around the county are pictured marching across Carfax with their banners and a police escort in May 1968.

Oxford Revolutionary Socialist Student demonstrators scuffle with proctors and bedels on their way to Convocation House in November 1968. They were demanding to be let into a meeting of Congregation, the parliament of the university, but were successfully repelled, with at least one ending up on the ground.

Opposite above: Oxford undergraduates gathered outside the Examination Schools in order to add their names to the list of hundreds of signatures collected against the Government's increase in fees for overseas students, February 1968.

Opposite below: Students, some of them in full academic dress, pictured at the beginning of the Michaelmas Term of 1968 setting fire to copies of the Proctors' Memorandum, a booklet setting out the rules and regulations relevant to undergraduates, which is handed out to university freshmen on their arrival in Oxford.

In January 1969 the police certainly had their work cut out dealing with the crowds of demonstrators massing outside the Town Hall in protest against Enoch Powell, who was in Oxford to address a meeting. There were many arrests that day, including a left-wing local clergyman who was charged with possessing an offensive weapon – a tin of peas in a string bag!

To close the chapter on a more peaceful note, Oxford-born actor Patrick Mower is shown here taking a break with co-star Madeline Hinde during the filming of *Doctors Wear Scarlet* at Worcester College in April 1969. Patrick Mower was a former Gladiators actor and member of the St John's Boys' Club.

5

DOMESTIC MATTERS

This picture, taken at the Homeless Families Unit at Slade Park in July 1963, is a startling reminder of the seriousness of homelessness in prosperous Oxford at this time, despite an extensive building campaign. The City Health Committee had recently asked the Housing Department to make more room available, since the Homeless Families Unit at Slade Park was full.

These council flats near the London Road roundabout at Headington, seen here nearing completion in September 1961, are classic examples of 1960s housing. Oxford only has two tower blocks, Plowman Towers at Marston and Foresters Tower at Wood Farm.

An icy scene in Town Furze estate, Headington, during the winter of 1962/3, before residents had had a chance to soften the bleak impression created by the bare concrete façades and featureless gardens.

The houses in Sunderland Avenue, North Oxford, shown here in the mid-1950s shortly after completion, are in a totally different part of the city and miles away from council estates, both socially and geographically.

This display at the Co-op's carpet department is typical of the vivid designs popular in 1961. In the days before open-plan living and central heating, householders would carpet each room in a different pattern rather than attempting to match or co-ordinate them, but at least this was an improvement on cold linoleum.

In the hamlet of Binsey, water was obtained from a well in buckets with the help of a windmill until running water arrived there in 1958. However, this was not installed in the residents' homes but had to be drawn from a standpipe on the green. Mrs Lund is pictured demonstrating the wonders of modern science to her daughter.

While an increasing number of Oxford residents were able to create their own little palaces, others didn't have a bath in their homes. When the new slipper and shower baths opened in Howard Street, East Oxford, in the spring of 1959, there was a queue of customers – most of them elderly – eager to use the six baths and four showers.

Mrs C. Peek, attendant and caretaker at the Howard Street baths, hands the first ticket and a towel to Councillor Bill Fagg, vice-chairman of the Baths Committee, who officially opened the £8,000 building. Charges were 6d for adults for a slipper bath (OAPs 4d) and 4d for a shower, while towels cost 3d and soap a penny.

Kettles, some of them whistlers, feature prominently in the electrical department of the Oxford and District Co-op in 1958. Electric blankets were very welcome in chilly bedrooms. Every home had a number of portable fires (the bowl-shaped one was common), which would be positioned wherever they were needed. The lamp on the counter would have been considered the height of fashion.

Alan Woodward's extensive window display, on the corner of Pembroke Street and St Ebbe's in 1959, shows that by this date household appliances had become widespread. The Flatley drier in the central window was a bargain at just under £9, but even so, hire purchase terms were available. Electrical neon signs were among the more unusual items being advertised.

Armchairs and occasional tables with typical 1960s legs were on show outside Walker's furniture shop in Headington in 1963. The long narrow shades on the standard lamps inside the shop are also very much of the period. Later, the council would clamp down on shops who displayed their goods and even A-boards on the pavement, charging them with causing an obstruction.

In 1959, Paramount Sewing Machines in the Cowley Road stocked both the traditional type of machine and the new electric ones, which were beginning to make an appearance. In the left-hand window, Father Christmas is suggesting a sewing machine as a present, as home sewing was still very common, both for furnishings and items of clothing.

Above: Chiltern Cleaners' new branch in the Cowley Road attracted a queue in 1959 when it gave away 5*s* vouchers for the first 250 orders worth more than 5*s*. The first 100 customers also received a special gift. Surprisingly, few of the customers appear to be bringing in larger items for cleaning.

Left: The Oxford colleges are home to their students for a good part of the year. In February 1960, cutting-edge technology included this top-loading washing machine, installed by the Junior Common Room at St Edmund Hall and fascinating these undergraduates. This inspired 'potential washermen' at the Queen's College to launch a campaign to buy one for their own Junior Common Room. However, drying, airing and ironing still remained a problem.

For those who felt like a change and had been inspired by the DIY television programmes which were starting around this time, Boswell's homeware department, featured here in 1961, offered a good choice of paints and varnishes with expert advice on hand. The assistant's white coat gives him a suitably scientific look.

After a hard day's work, many people liked to go home and relax by listening to the radio, playing records or watching television. The Coronation in 1953 had brought television to the attention of British viewers. One of the leading stockists of all types of home entertainment was Russell Acott, on the corner of High Street and Alfred Street, shown here in October 1963.

In the 1960s, as today, a favourite form of home-improvement was gardening. This photograph of cutting-edge lawnmowers, taken in 1964, was used as an advertisement for the new showroom at Curtis and Horn's Park End Street premises. The business was famous for its agricultural machinery.

Opposite above: In this close-up of Leech and Hainge's window display in Headington, in December 1963, the ever-present transistor radios are very much in evidence. The record sleeves on display show that Shirley Bassey and Harry Secombe were popular, despite Beatle-mania. Apart from two LPs of seasonal music, there is no sign of any Christmas decorations.

Opposite below: In East Oxford, Pickett's, a very long-established Oxford company, stocked similar items to Russell Acott. In this picture from 1963, the assistant is demonstrating a radiogram. These combinations of radios and record-players were sold as attractive items of furniture as well as being functional. Pickett's stocked all the leading makes of the time, and, as usual, hire purchase was available.

Despite increasingly strong competition from wireless, television, and recorded music throughout the 1950s, reading was still one of the most common leisure activities. In 1959, when this picture was taken, paperback sales had reached an unprecedented high. Most of the magazines on display on this stall in the Covered Market have long ceased publication.

One of the most important aspects of home life is of course the preparation and eating of meals. There were still plenty of smaller, specialist stockists about like Vallis's bakery in Quarry High Street, Headington, shown here in the 1950s. Vallis's also had a shop in Old High Street, Headington.

Over the years small businesses gave way to larger ones offering a variety of foodstuffs under one roof, as well as nearby parking. As early as 1957, Mr L. Cox, manager of the Co-op's self-service butchery department on Cowley Road, was explaining the hygienic advantages of buying sealed meat.

After being tempted by all the white goods which surrounded her in 1959, this housewife has decided to invest in a fridge from Boswell's home-ware department. At this period freezers were limited to a small section at the top of the fridge. The one the assistant is demonstrating has a larger freezer compartment than was usual.

Grimbly Hughes & Co. Ltd, photographed in 1959 in its Cornmarket premises, where it was first established in 1840. As Oxford's answer to Fortnum & Mason, it was known for its cheese and bacon counters, and orders for its Christmas hampers came from all over the world. In 1961 the business relocated round the corner to Queen Street.

Despite its move to Queen Street, Grimbly Hughes closed two years later when the parent company, Jacksons of Piccadilly, disposed of the lease. Apart from the fact that such an institution was to close after all those years, the idea of a 20 per cent discount on all stock must have struck the people of Oxford as very strange.

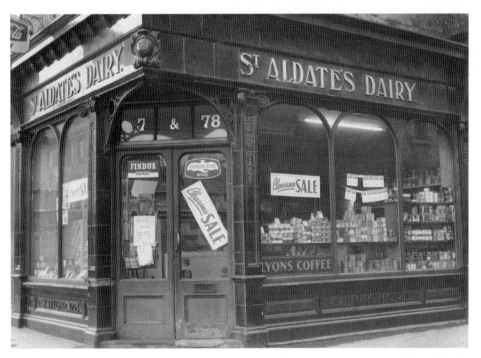

According to its managing director, Mr Wigmore, the closure of the 100-year-old St Aldate's Dairy in December 1965 was blamed on parking restrictions, which deterred passing trade. Before the war, the green-tiled grocer's sold eggs, butter, milk and cream, then it started to sell groceries, which turned it into a thriving little business, but by the mid-1960s this was no longer viable.

Up in Headington, a privately-owned supermarket was doing well despite the opposition from the chains. Norman Allen's shop, which started off as a butcher's in Old High Street, evolved into a full-scale supermarket on the London Road, shown here in 1963. Most of the items displayed on the shelves are no longer in production.

An example of the attraction of the large chains, which were gradually putting the small local food shops out of business by the mid-1960s. This is Woolworth's new chilled and frozen food section and the delicatessen counter as they were in October 1966, when English beef was still a very desirable product.

These very basic checkouts at one of Butler's supermarkets, situated immediately next door to Tesco in the Cowley Road, were photographed in 1962. This store was part of the country-wide explosion of supermarkets that year – it was estimated that around 750 stores were opened, with an additional 5,000 expected to open in the next decade.

This was the era of the cocktail cabinet and Chianti bottle in straw containers. Also popular were 'miniatures' and lady-like drinks such as snowballs and Babycham. An assistant at the Cowley Road branch of Frank Twining's wine shop gives a customer advice on buying suitable wines for Christmas in 1963.

In December 1963, G&C Hobbs at No. 128 Oxford Road, Cowley, put on this fine display of fancy biscuits, giant boxes of chocolates, tinned fruit and even Christmas stockings containing a selection of chocolate treats. The personal relationship still found in family shops like this one is evidenced by the string of Christmas cards from customers.

For those who didn't have time to cook or simply couldn't be bothered, there was always the local chippy, like this one in Walton Street, which displays the menu and prices current in 1968. Del Nevo's, which was one of the oldest and best known in Oxford, also offered a home-delivery service. Like all other fish shops at the time, it was closed on Mondays because there was no delivery of fresh fish on Sundays.

6

VANISHING OXFORD

Carfax Assembly Rooms, shown here in October 1962, was the heart of entertainment in Oxford, even playing host to The Beatles before they became famous nationally. The site, which included a self-service café and snack bar, was taken over by the Midland Bank and is now the HSBC Bank.

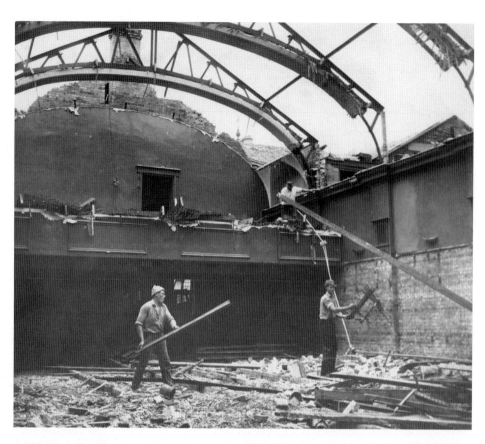

This long-established shop in Market Street, pictured here in 1966, was pulled down to make way for the construction of a service area leading into the Covered Market. Fortunately, the name C.H. Brown & Son lives on in a very successful leather and saddlery business inside the Covered Market.

Opposite above: Workmen demolishing the Forum dance hall in High Street in July 1965. Many Oxonians of a certain age will have fond memories of the hall, which was part of the Masonic complex, the temple of which was dedicated in 1907. The last dance to be held in the Forum was in June 1965 and after closure it was replaced by an extension to St Edmund Hall, which cost £500,000.

Opposite below: In 1958 a temporary wooden footbridge was put up by the site of the International Tea Company's shop in High Street to allow piping to pass underneath. Both the International and Sainsbury's have since disappeared from the High Street, the latter having relocated to the Westgate Centre.

Demolition in progress on the gymnasium at the Bear Lane end of Alfred Street in 1965. The building, where many Oxford University boxers did their training, made way for an extension to the Westminster Bank. Amusing sketches of undergraduate gymnasts can be found in Cuthbert Bede's *The Adventures of Mr Verdant Green*.

An air-raid shelter, which had long outlived its usefulness at St Clement's School, was finally knocked down in 1959. The steel ball, which was used to smash up concrete and sections of brick wall, weighed nearly two tons and must have delighted any small boys who were allowed near enough to watch it in action.

Demolition in Cambridge Street to make room for the new Oxford Magistrates' Courts at St Ebbe's, June 1966. Tom Tower can be glimpsed in the background. The area which Cambridge Street occupied was later the subject of an archaeological dig.

This piece of artwork from the old School of Technology, Art and Commerce in St Ebbe's was found among the debris when the building was pulled down in 1959. Along with the Schools of Engineering, Architecture and Building, the School of Technology, Art and Commerce moved to Headington, where they evolved into the Oxford Polytechnic, which in turn became Oxford Brookes University.

Above: In 1960 scaffolding and a corrugated iron barrier surrounding the site of demolition work in St Ebbe's, near the junction with Queen Street, collapsed and fell across the road. Although the road had been open to traffic and people were walking along it on their way to work, nobody was injured.

Left: The remains of thirteenth-century buildings used by the community of Dominican, or Black Friars, were uncovered in the part of St Ebbe's which was traditionally known as 'The Friars'. This discovery was made during an archaeological dig in an area bounded by Speedwell Street, Cambridge Terrace and the former Cambridge Street in 1967.

This old brick chimney belonging to the Swan Bakery in Paradise Street was blown up in 1964. The site was earmarked for the city's largest office block, costing an estimated £500,000. Paradise Street and Paradise Square take their names from the 'paradise' or garden of the Grey Friars. The word paradise, which means a walled enclosure, comes from Persia.

A church in Blackfriars' Road, dedicated to the Holy Trinity, was consecrated in 1845 to cater for residents of the warren of closely-packed streets in St Ebbe's. Holy Trinity was renovated and improved in 1893 only to be closed in 1954 and united with the parish of St Aldate's. Reminiscent of the *Marie Celeste*, on the church's closure, water remained in the tank for the hot water system and the numbers of the last hymns sung were still displayed in the frame above the pulpit.

The interior of Holy Trinity Church during demolition in 1957. Although closed due to its 'dangerous and dilapidated condition', it was occasionally used for weddings and christenings while regular services were held in the parish hall or the chapel of the Church Army Hostel. Although some of the slates had been corroded by sulphur from the gasworks, and the floorboards were chopped up for firewood, Holy Trinity contained much material that was sold for salvage.

Castle Street as it was in 1960 with shops, offices and pubs, when St Ebbe's was still a close and vibrant neighbourhood, despite the semi-slum condition of its streets. Its residents were moved up to Headington, where they were given newly-built homes.

The Oxford County Court building at the top of Castle Street, March 1968. Shortly after this photograph was taken, the court relocated to a site between St Ebbe's and St Aldate's. This site is now occupied by the Westgate Library. The mock-Tudor pub in the background, on the corner of Paradise Street, has been subject to several changes of name, but is currently the Castle Tavern.

The imposing redbrick Salvation Army Citadel, which was very much a local landmark, is shown to the left of the background of this photograph taken of Castle Street in 1967. Opened in 1888, the citadel was another victim of the redevelopment of St Ebbe's.

A view along an empty Castle Street in August 1967, which clearly shows it as it appeared before its realignment into the totally different street we know today. The tower in the right distance belongs to St Ebbe's Church.

The last building standing on the former canal wharf was the headquarters of Oxford City Sea Cadet Corps, which was demolished in 1956. The pub sign in the doorway is from the adjacent Queen's Arms, later renamed Rosie O'Grady's. Much of the redevelopment of the wharf had been done in the 1930s for the erection of Nuffield College, although work was suspended during the war. The area is now Worcester Street car park.

CHEAP
EVENING TRIPS
Depart
OXFORD LMS
3·55 P.M.

BLETCHLEY
WOLVERTON
NORTHAMPTON
RUGBY
COVENTRY

The London, Midland & Scottish railway station, which stood at the junction of Park End Street and Rewley Road, was built in 1851 by the designers of the Crystal Palace and incorporated some of the same cast-iron units in the canopy. It closed to passengers in 1951 and after a chequered history was taken to a museum at Quainton, Buckinghamshire. In this picture it obscures the nearby Great Western Railway station, which occupied approximately the same site as the present one.

Old houses coming down in a well-known part of the city centre in 1957. This is Chain Alley, which once linked George Street and Gloucester Green. The single-storey building to the right of the picture is the Municipal Restaurant and snack bar, one of several in the city opened to provide reasonably priced meals. This one was very convenient for the Gloucester Green bus station.

The Oxford branch of the Young Men's Christian Association stood at the far end of Walton Street until it was demolished in the summer of 1966. There is no longer a branch of the YMCA in Oxford today, although by a strange coincidence the England and Wales Head Office of the YWCA is at Clarendon House in Cornmarket.

On Boxing Day 1899, folklorist and musicologist Cecil Sharp watched a side of unemployed local workmen giving a display of Morris dancing at Sandfield Cottage, London Road, Headington. Sharp wrote down the tunes to their dances and added them to his collection and 50 Sandfield Cottage became important in the history of English Morris. The house, which later became the home of dog-handler Barbara ('Walkies') Woodhouse was demolished in 1965 for the construction of Horwood Close.

The demolition and clearance work began on the site of what was to become the Cowley Centre (now Templars Square) in 1960. Although this part of Cowley is better known for its shopping centres, part of old Cowley village, centred round the parish church of St James, survives and is now a conservation area.

The last occupied house in a terrace of four in Between Towns Road, stands forlornly next to its derelict neighbours awaiting demolition in the summer of 1961. When their new home was ready for them, the family moved out and the construction company building the new Cowley Centre on the site were able to move in.

Still in Cowley, the old Community Centre in Barns Road was pulled down in 1964. The new centre on the other side of the road was completed at a cost of £75,000. Apart from the usual meetings, dances and bingo sessions, it was used by Oxford College of Further Education for several years before the completion of the purpose-built college in Oxpens Road.

The demolition of a further five houses in Between Towns Road followed in 1966 in order to widen a section of the road between Cowley Parish Hall and Cowley Workers' Club. It was found necessary to make it into a dual carriageway and involved major road works, which took six months. The City Engineer's Department stated that throughout this disruption, which involved the post office, the gas and electricity supplies, the road would remain open to traffic.

A strange sort of demolition took place at Cowley Centre when The Nelson, the area's new local, was pulled down in 1970 to make way for an extension to the adjacent Sainsbury's store. However, it was rebuilt a mere 20 yards away, with a frontage on Between Towns Road and all the up-to-date attractions that a modern pub could offer.

Other titles published by The History Press

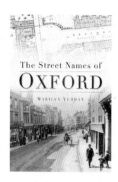

The Street Names of Oxford

MARILYN YURDAN

This book traces the origins of names found in Oxford, not only of its streets and road, villages, suburbs and housing estates, but also of the various colleges which make up t university, many of which have had a considerable influence on its streets. The illustratio range in date from nineteenth-century prints and old pictures to new photographs whi show a much-changed city.

978 0 7509 5098 5

Oxford In Old Photographs

ROBERT S. BLACKHAM

This collection provides a comprehensive guide to Oxford's past, using rare images of t city to bring a bygone era to life. Focusing on the architecture that has existed for centuri yet remains impressive today, many of Oxford's celebrated landmarks, including the famo university buildings, are fully explored by over 200 vintage pictures. These are accompani by informative and revealing captions which provide little-known information about t characters responsible for the development of Oxford up until the present day.

978 0 7524 5128 2

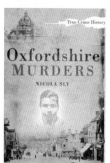

Oxfordshire Murders

NICOLA SLY

Oxfordshire Murders brings together twenty-five murderous tales, some which were litt known outside the county, and others which made national headlines. They includ the deaths of two gamekeepers, brutally murdered in 1824 and 1835; Henrietta Walke killed by her husband at Chipping Norton in 1887; Mary Allen, shot by Harry Rowl at Cassington in the same year; and Anne Kempson, murdered by Henry Seymour, door-to-door salesman, in Oxford in 1931.

978 0 7524 5359 0

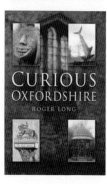

Curious Oxfordshire

ROGER LONG

Curious Oxfordshire is a guide to over 100 unusual and extraordinary sights, incidents an legends from all parts of the county. Featured here are tales of unsolved murders, witchcraf hangings, poltergeists, underground caves and passages, 'cunning men', backswording an riots. From an unconventional exorcism performed with a bicycle pump to the tail o a vast shark pointing skywards from a Headington roof, this book will make fascinating reading for all those interested in the quirky and strange side of Oxfordshire.

978 0 7509 4957 6

Visit our website and discover thousands of other History Press books.

www.thehistorypress.co.uk